LEADERSHIP

THE COURAGE TO LEAD

Idea-rich team empowerment

Bob 'Idea Man' Hooey
Author, Legacy of Leadership

4th edition – updated 2023

Special thanks to all those who have encouraged me in my leadership journey over the years. Too many to credit here, but I so appreciate you.

Thanks to my wife and creative partner, Irene Gaudet, who helps me create each of my publications and ensures they create value.

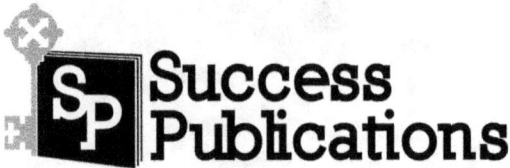

SP Success Publications

Box 10, Egremont, Alberta, Canada T0A0Z0
www.SuccessPublications.ca

"I have been so excited working with Bob Hooey, as he has given inspiration and motivation to our leadership team members. Both at the Brick Warehouse – Alberta and here at Art Van Furniture – Michigan; with his years of experience in working with business executives and his humorous and delightful packaging of his material, he makes learning with Bob a real joy. But most importantly, **anyone who encounters his material is the better for it.***"*
Kim Yost, CEO Art Van Furniture (retired), former CEO The Brick

- **Motivate your teams**, your employees, and your leaders to 'productively' grow and 'profitably' succeed!
- **Protect your conference investment** - leverage your training dollars.
- **Enhance your professional career** and sell more products and services.
- **Equip and motivate your leaders** and their teams to grow and succeed, 'even' in tough times!
- **Leverage your time** to enhance your skills, equip your teams, and better serve your clients.
- **Leverage your leadership** and investment of time to leave a significant legacy!

Call today to engage best-selling author, award winning, inspirational leadership keynote speaker, leaders' success coach, and employee development trainer, Bob 'Idea Man' Hooey and his innovative, audience based, results-focused, Ideas At Work! for your next company, convention, leadership, staff, training, or association event. You'll be glad you did!

Call 1-780-736-0009 to connect with **Bob 'Idea Man' Hooey** today!
Learn more about Bob at: www.ideaman.net or www.BobHooey.training

Getting started...

Welcome to the journey of an evolving career and management focus on personal leadership and engaged coaching. Change in global perspective has placed a new focus and pressure on finding and applying more productive uses of our assets and updating our employees' skills to compete successfully. Taking personal leadership in your own career growth and success is worth the investment. This is where you apply 'leverage' to dynamically succeed!

Having the courage to lead is the starting point to upward mobility and success. Acting on it is next!

There is an increased acceptance to using personal leadership and engaged coaching in the workplace. In the past, coaching has been regulated or known only as a remedial method of helping employees improve 'sagging' or deficient performance. It still has a valid use in this area. In recent history, workplace coaching has a new focus. Employees, managers, and executives have been experiencing positive results from enlisting the help of a **leadership coach** to help them improve in specific areas or to achieve specific goals. People have been going 'outside' the corporate arena and enlisting or recruiting personal or leadership coaches. **They want to change, to improve their performance, and to enhance their ability to win! This book can be a guide in that process and quest.**

Top performing leaders, executives, and managers have seen the wisdom and a positive return on their investment of time and resources in training and coaching their employees for 'optimal' results. Things are changing in boardrooms, and on the sales floors of businesses across North America and around the globe. The author has worked with leaders and their teams across to world and has seen this firsthand.

People experience problems and challenges in their performance for four major reasons:

Poor or inadequate training for the job

Inadequate equipment to do the job

Time constraints to do the job

Motivation to do the job

Leadership coaching in its essence, will help discover the area(s) which are acting as roadblocks for the person being coached. Leadership coaching can help turn roadblocks into stepping-stones for increased success, productivity, and a real sense of satisfaction on the job.

Leadership coaching can bring a sense of satisfaction to the coach too – in bringing out the best, and in seeing your people win!

It takes courage to lead, but it is so worth it to see your own growth and the growth and success of those you lead. Check out some of these idea-rich team empowerment strategies. Go for it!

When covid-19 hit in early 2020 leaders around the globe had the challenge to pivot to on-line virtual communication and engagement.

Bob was one of those leaders making the pivot to change a 2-day live event in Barcelona into an online one virtually over night.

Bob 'Idea Man' Hooey, Certified Virtual Presenter
www.ideaman.net
www.BobHooey.training
+1-780-736-0009

"Outstanding leaders go out of the way to boost the self-esteem of their personnel. If people believe in themselves, it's amazing what they can accomplish."
Sam Walton, founder of Walmart and Sam's Club

Table of Contents

"One of the most important things for any leader is to never let anyone else define who you are. And you define who you are. I never think of myself as being a woman CEO of this company. I think of myself as a steward of a great institution."
Ginni Rometty, CEO of IBM

Leadership observations

"Learning is the essential fuel for leaders, the source of high-octane energy that keeps up the momentum by continually sparking new understanding, new ideas, and new challenges. It is indispensable under today's conditions of rapid change and complexity. Very simply, those who do not learn do not long survive as leaders."
Warren Bevis & Burt Nanus

A few thoughts on leadership drawn from observations and lessons learned first-hand from a wide range of leaders. I have been blessed with some great role models – leaders in business; industry; association management; community service; Toastmasters; my NSA, CAPS, and GSF colleagues; and even from my parents and friends. Here are some shared characteristics observed from the leaders in my life.

Leaders are not born.
Leaders emerge and can be nurtured by other leaders who see their potential. Leadership is a learned skill honed by experience, and by finding the inner motivational points that inspire people to take it in various aspects of their lives. Leaders are revealed when people see value and follow their direction. I saw this first-hand in my Toastmasters and CAPS leadership when I approached people and asked them to tackle a challenge. They often took personal leadership and championed its eventual success.

Leaders are open to change and have the courage to do so.
Positive change often happens when someone takes personal leadership and responsibility in a situation. Leaders develop a sense of adventure and a realization that change is not always a negative event. Leaders see themselves as catalysts for innovative change. A true leader will see the plateau or status quo as an opportunity or foundation to move ahead and make positive changes.

Leaders are creative and flexible in finding solutions to common challenges.
Often it is the creative approach that shows the way out of the problem or mess at hand. The leader looks for that creative or innovative 'twist' which will unlock the secret to solving the challenge at hand. They are persistent in looking for innovative ways to solve problems and will inspire others to do the same.

Leaders make mistakes and build on those lessons learned.

Life is about learning and leadership even more so. Leaders take calculated risks, and sometimes they make mistakes or fail. That is a part of the leadership process! The difference being, leaders understand this, and learn from the experience. They will move ahead, better informed for the next opportunity to learn.

Leaders are forged in the heat of reality and moulded on the anvil of adversity by the hammers of life.

Personal leadership emerges in the heat of the worst challenges and conditions in your life. You have a choice to take personal responsibility for your role and abilities to act. I have seen the most unlikely leaders take this role when the going was tough or the odds overwhelming – and succeed where others simply complained or quit trying. Leaders don't quit; they simply find the strength and keep going.

Leaders are readers.
This may not be true of every leader. Many of those I have grown to respect, make reading a definite part of their leadership growth path. They read outside their own areas and are open to learn from a myriad of sources. They have found that in a multitude of counsel there is wisdom. Reading allows you to access the wisdom of the ages from leaders long gone, and from current and emerging leaders. Selective reading provides information that allows you to explore new ideas, new methods, new ways of thinking and gives you the ammunition you need to set and reach your goals.

Leaders are the foundation upon which our success is given substance.
In my life, this is true! I can look back to the pivotal points in my life and often there was the guiding hand of a leader who invested in my life, my growth, and my well-being. My guess is you might see something similar in your life and career.

So many people played a role in honing my talents, enhancing my skills, and allowing me to discover that I had leadership hidden inside. I have been humbled by their investment, encouragement, and the recognition I have garnered along the way. My continued leadership is my gift back to them for the faith they showed in my life. Leadership is a 'giving back' lifestyle choice and commitment.

Leadership skills are changing... are yours?

If you truly seek to be an effective 21st century leader, a reflective look at this list of leadership styles, activities or attributes would be a wise investment.

Use these questions as an informal leadership audit and a checklist on how you measure up.

Ask yourself how many of these you exhibit, as you seek to lead those who have entrusted you with their concerns?

- **What needs to change?**
- **When will you act to change?**
- **Who will you ask for help?**

Responsible

Do you take full responsibility for your actions and decisions? Do you also take responsibility for your team's results? Responsibility, regardless if those results are positive or negative. Leaders support and stand behind the actions of those they lead. No avoidance or evasiveness!

Growing

Are you a leader, on the grow, who is committed to seeking out new ideas, new methods, and new alliances to help serve those you lead? Are you a leader who is also a reader? Leaders exhibit an increased appetite to learn and find out how things work!

Exemplary

Do you walk your talk? Do your motives, actions, and attitudes reflect the character you would honestly like to see developed? People will follow your lead when you walk your talk and lead by example.

Inspiring

Do you inspire confidence and trust in those who follow you? Can you call them to action, in solving your mutual challenges? Remember, if no one follows you, you are a leader in name only. Leadership is a lifestyle, not a label. If they see it in your actions, it will translate to their own actions.

Efficient

How are you on using your time wisely and 'leveraging' the time of those you serve? Do they see you using your time in productive activities on their behalf? Do you have time to fully do your job, enhance your career, or lead your team to increased success?

Caring

Do your people know from experience that you care about them? Do you model it? Someone once told me, *"They will not care how much you know, until they know how much you care!"* When they can see your commitment to them, they will follow you through hell and high water to succeed.

Communicating

How are you at sharing your ideas, at listening to the needs and concerns of your people, and in making sure that you fully understand them? Do you make sure they are well informed about what the challenges and your proposed solutions to those changes entail? Have you taken training to enhance your communication skills?

Goal oriented

Are you a leader who is effective in setting realistic goals, communicating those goals, and gathering people to support the attainment of those goals? Above all, are you a leader who achieves the worthwhile goals set for the common good?

Decisive

Can you make an informed decision and quickly act on that decision? Do you study a challenge to death and continually put off making a decision while waiting for more information? There are times when a decision has to be made without all of the facts – are you willing to do so?

Competent

This strikes at the heart of your ability to deliver the goods for your people. Are you competent to do the job and do it well? This is where you walk your talk and lead by example. They have to see it to believe it! If they see your expertise or competence, they are more open to your coaching or critiquing them in their roles. They may just put your ideas into action too!

Unifying

Are you a leader who seeks to include everyone involved and works hard to make sure no-one is excluded? Are you a leader who builds bonds between diverse groups, many with conflicting agendas and viewpoints? Are you a leader who can earn their trust and allow them to get past their divisiveness to get behind you in accomplishing something which is for everyone's best interest? Are you a catalyst for commitment?

Working

Are you a leader who is committed to working on behalf of those who trust you? A leader who is not afraid to get their hands dirty, to dig in and lead by example, to do what is needed to get the job done successfully? Are you a leader who sets an energetic pace and is fully engaged on working out the solutions and to engaging people in the partnership of performance in achieving common goals?

Tough list, isn't it? But, if you would truly seek to be a 21st century leader, these are the skills that will assist you in successfully serving and leading your people. Are you willing to change and challenge your growth?

Change is a creative leadership choice

"Searching for the peak performer within yourself has one basic meaning - You recognize yourself as a person who was born, not as a peak performer but as a learner. With the capacity to grow, change, and reach for the highest possibilities of human nature, you regard yourself as a person in process. Not perfect, but a person who keeps asking: What more can I be? What else can I achieve that will benefit my company and myself? That will contribute to my family and my community?"
Charles Garfield

In life, we have the opportunity thrust upon us to make changes and to take personal leadership in dealing with those changes. A death, a major illness, or a major economic upheaval can force us to take stock of our lives at that point, and make sometimes-radical changes; to take leadership in our own lives and the lives of those we love, lead or work with daily.

As competition becomes more global in our changing economy, we find businesses and professional associations being stretched and tested. Staffing has become more challenging, and so has training and marketing.

Customers are becoming more demanding and specific in what they want. Change is pushed on us everywhere we turn. We can avoid change, can't we? That's what too many business leaders think and miss their full potential.

Isn't it better to seize the opportunities to change and grow? Isn't it better to be a leader who is open to learn, stretch, and to push yourself and your team past your own comfort zones? Isn't it better to lead than follow in the dust?

This change is a creative leadership choice! Life is a series of changes and choices, why not take personal leadership and control their direction and pace? Why not decide to be a leader, not a follower!

Ask yourself a few questions. Allow your honest reactions to reflect the changes in your attitudes, and the actions that may need to be addressed to maximize your life, your career advancement and leadership performance. **Change is the breakfast of leadership – applied risk has its rewards!**

What do I really want to have my life to accomplish? What is my biggest dream?

What would I like my organization/company to accomplish? Where do I want my career to go?

Looking back from retirement, I am most proud of _____?

What am I afraid of? What is stopping me?

What keeps me up at night?

What do I need to change to make it work? When do I need to change it?

When will I commit to start making these changes?

Will you have the courage to change? Will you commit to being your best, and to applying your leadership in creatively building your business or association to maximize its potential? Tough questions, aren't they?

Remember the words of retailer **J.C. Penney**: *"No one need live a minute longer as he/she is, because the creator endowed us with the ability to change ourselves."*

Answering these questions will have given you a 'glimpse' of what needs to be changed to make your dreams, teams, and goals a reality. The secret is in putting foundations under your dreams and actions under your goals. The secret to unlocking your 'leadership' potential is in accessing your ability to embrace and utilize change for mutual benefit. The choice is yours!

"Of all the things I've done, the most vital is coordinating those who work with me and aiming their efforts at a certain goal."
Walt Disney, founder of Disney

Qualities of an EFFECTIVE Leader, Trainer or Coach

In today's changing economic landscape, leaders often move into the coaching role. Becoming a good coach means learning to draw on your abilities and skills to train those who need your help. Here are some **traits of successful and effective leaders, trainers, and coaches.** How do you measure up? Are there skills where you could use a little training or coaching yourself?

Good Communications Skills

- Use clear and concise language to instruct, direct, and coach.
- Use your active listening skills.
- Maintain eye contact.

Solid understanding of the subject

- Comprehensive understanding of the subject or skills.
- Willingness to draw from your background.
- Willingness to grow and update your professional development.

Experience

- It helps if you have done the job personally.
- Previous experience in training.

Patience

- New people can make mistakes while they learn.
- It often takes a few tries to get it right.
- Remember how it was for you when you started out?

Interest in being a trainer or coach

- You need to enjoy helping people.
- Seeing people grow and learn makes you feel good.
- Seeing others' success gives you a sense of pride and satisfaction.

Genuine respect for other people

- People view you as being knowledgeable.
- People view you as being trustful and trustworthy.

Well-developed sense of humor

- You see the humor in the situation.
- You don't take yourself or life too seriously.

Having these traits and skills won't 'guarantee' your success as a leader, trainer, or coach. They will, however, give you a better chance to do the job effectively. They will also give you an 'edge' in helping your team grow and succeed.

"Management is doing things right; leadership is doing the right things." *Peter F. Drucker, author and educator*

Observing and measuring performance
Keys to effective leadership coaching

If you are truly dedicated to helping those you lead to improve their on-the-job performance and productivity, it helps to observe them in action. Then you will be in a better position to guide their growth.

Professional coaches in the athletic arena use on site observation and video replays. This allows them to isolate and work on specific areas, techniques, or skills which need improvement. Leaders who watch and listen are better equipped to teach and to share insights to assist their team members enhance their performance.

In the business world, these 'instant replays' can at times be filtered or edited by the people reporting them to the leader, coach, or manager. It is difficult to know how well they are doing without personally observing or tracking their performance. Better systems and better information gathering can lead to a better result and better coaching by the leadership team.

Successful leaders and managers look at both the results and the process to find areas where they can assist their team members fine tune or 'tweak' their skills for enhanced performance and productivity.

Performance observation and measurements must be done on a regular, reoccurring basis to offer ongoing validity in your leadership coaching efforts.

Learning how to observe your team without making them feel intimidated or uncomfortable is a skill you'll need to acquire as you evolve your leadership and coaching expertise.

Coaches Donna Berry, Charles Cadwell and Joe Fehrman suggest these tips for observation. I include them here, along with my own observations, for your consideration. Use them as a guide, as you plan your leadership/ coaching efforts, and seek to enhance your ability to effectively lead your team.

How to Observe

Observe the process used.

You want to be able to re-design or improve the process; so all your team leverages the lessons.

Observe result.

- What is happening because of this action?
- What is supposed to be happening?
- Why is there a gap?

Therefore, personal observation gives you better insights to be able to help them improve and to help you improve your systems too.

Explain why you are observing (to help them improve!)

They need to know you are not there to catch them 'messing up' but to look for ways to help them be more productive in what they do!

Don't interrupt workflow.

- Unless you need a specific answer or clarification – let them do their job.
- Observe and record the process and the results. Watch the full cycle of what they do!

Ask questions to verify your understanding.

Where needed, ask them to explain what they are doing, or what they understand to do. This might be the coaching aspect of your role as a leader if you observe them doing something dramatically different than the norm.

Watch operation several times.

This allows you to get a sense of the process and the flow for evaluation. Repetition can be revealing.

Make notes for discussion.

Don't rely on your memory. Don't make your note taking an obvious thing as that might add additional stress.

Compare observations with any written or 'normal' procedures

Observe others on team for comparison purposes.

See how other team members in a similar role are doing. This can help you in improving the process and potentially showing where one team member might have a misunderstanding or a training issue.

Be aware of your influence on the employee's performance.

Remember how you felt when someone was watching you do something and take that into account? Even champions can find this a challenge.

Helping your team to grow will require strategic and insightful work on your part.

It will require time to observe their performance, to design systems to help measure their performance, and to allow you to give them the positive, helpful feedback they need.

It will also show you where your own recruitment, orientation, and training or ongoing professional development efforts are solid, and where they need work to ensure your ongoing productivity in this competitive world market.

It is hard work! But your visible and positive investment in their growth will pay dividends in the future. Dividends in increased performance, improved morale, and team building, and in enhanced productivity and profits.

A guide to the care and feeding of new team members... The first 90 days

"You may have the loftiest goals, the highest ideals, the noblest dreams, but remember this, nothing works unless you do."
Nido Qubein

Adding someone new to your team is very much like a first date. Both parties are a little anxious and eager to please, and sometimes it turns out the same way. There are a few guidelines that I have found timely and helpful, both as a manager, as a new recruit, and more recently as a business leadership coach with my various clients around North America and across the globe.

As an employer, leader, or manager, you have a lot riding on the decision to recruit. Money and time invested aside, your leadership, reputation, company, or department is on the line, along with the working relationships already established with your current team. It can easily cost you up to six months wages to train an employee in the extra time spent supervising, training and in lost time or mistakes.

As a new recruit, you too have some risk, in the time invested to learn new products, procedures, or services and build a new client base.

Wouldn't it be a good idea to work at creating a partnership that allows both parties to win? With the major investment of 'time', I would hope both parties would be open to working together in making it a successful partnership that would grow more productive over time.

One of my basic foundations for success in any 'working' partnership is to be clear and realistic in laying out your new role and fully understanding its related responsibilities. Nothing frustrates as much as not knowing what to do or looking dumb when you have missed something that "everyone else knows but forgot to let you in on the secret or the way we do it here!"

Being realistic in laying out a time-line for "learning and assimilating" before establishing firm goals is important too. This needs to be tailored to the expertise and aptitude of each new recruit. Leaders and employers, tough as it seems, "you treat them all the same by treating them differently." Each individual needs specific guidance and coaching.

As the employer, leader, trainer, or coach, you should work to establish an environment to encourage questions and asking for help. This saves time, frustration, and mistakes and helps build a positive relationship that will make your partnership grow.

To get the most out of your latest recruit or volunteer, follow these helpful hints. Leadership coaching in a corporate or business environment or the volunteer sector can be an effective tool and draws on these guidelines.

Define the position carefully.
What are the new recruit's responsibilities – in each area of their position? To be effective, what skills, knowledge, and attitudes must be displayed? Be as clear and specific as you can. It will set the tone and foundation for eventual success for yourself and your new team member. Revise as needed to reflect changing roles.

Hire selectively.
Hiring people who have pre-training reduces your own time and resource investment. Investigate who trains people with the skills you need and call them. Selection from a pool of properly trained (training programs or schools) or depth of experience (your competitors) can help you get a leg up in your productivity and profits too!

Be specific about where each employee needs improvement.
Can the lack of performance be 'fixed' through training? (Sometimes it's motivation or personal problems.) Clearly communicate these areas and offer your support. Don't be afraid to spell out the consequences, if the deficiency in their performance remains unchanged over time.

Provide ongoing support and encouragement.
Assist your team in selecting and undertaking specific training and professional development. Investing in their growth often returns large dividends.

Measure and communicate results.
Don't be afraid to hold your team accountable for reasonable expectations and responsibilities that have been well communicated. Check to see if training has reduced or eliminated the recruit's skill or knowledge deficiency, and/or they are equipped to make a better contribution to your company.

Do this in a timely and constructive manner.
Set aside regular, uninterrupted time to discuss training and performance issues. You shouldn't have to wait until the 90-grace period has expired to ask

for changes in performance or to offer critiques. **Do it now!**

If you are selective in who you recruit and diligent in the time you invest together; you will see your investment pay handsomely in contributing productive employees or team members who add value to your firm and use their new skills for everyone's benefit.

One training tip would be to standardise as much as possible of your business, its procedures, systems, and 'special challenges' or activities. This will be a great help in getting new recruits up to speed. This is also a great way to keep current team members up to speed. Make sure it is a work in progress. Enlist your current staff in its creation and upkeep. This is a great way to build and maintain your working relationship and foster a sense of partnership.

But what happens if you are a seasonal employer and your training time is shorter? How do you make the best of your training time and maximise your investment? How do I hire good staff? That is an important factor to keep in mind when you are interviewing. Making sure you pick those open to work and learn on the job is important; but after they are on board, then what?

Jeremy Pinder from Australia said, *"Because I am in the recruitment business, I get calls on a regular basis asking, "where can I find good staff". It annoys me, but I just tell them that they are asking the wrong question. What they should be asking is "how do I take the staff that I've got and make them better?"* Good change of perspective with great results!

My friend and fellow speaker **Bill Marvin**, The Restaurant Doctor from Washington had this to say, *"You already have the kind of people you need. If they are not performing up to your standards, whose fault is it? They asked for a job, you gave it to them! You need to look at who is responsible for performance? If you place the burden on the staff, you are at their mercy. It is not going to change until they change. However, if you accept that your job – maybe your most important job – is staff development. Then training and performance become YOUR responsibility, and that you can do something about!"*

My challenge to you as leaders, managers and employers is to look at the cost of having untrained or poorly trained team members in lost business, or unhappy customers.

- **How much is each customer worth to your business?**

- **How much are you willing to risk in poor training efforts?**

In our customer service seminars, I have audiences work this out – then I hit them with the truth – based on proven statistics each unhappy customer costs you up to value of sixteen. The unhappy customer doesn't return, tells at least 10 people about his unsatisfactory experience, and doesn't tell the 5 people about a happy experience as would be expected. It can really add up!

Investing time and money in protecting your investment and the reputation of your business or organization is a good investment. It is tough to look at spending the time training people who may only be with you for a season. But if you are honest with yourself, you will see it is an investment that must be made if your organization is to grow and flourish.

Taking advantage of training systems is a good investment. One thing I've learned is the importance of not reinventing the wheel. Check out what is available from local agencies and correspondence training programs. There are programs for leaders, employers, and employees in various industries.

For example, The Canadian Tourism Human Resource Council has developed a comprehensive series of training programs videos and materials. They are a great source of standardizing your training and staff skill sets. Contact them at (613) 213-6949 or cthrc@cthrc.ca for information on how you can access these materials or your local Tourism Education Council. McGraw-Hill Ryerson has some good training materials as well. Call: 1-800-565-5758

Looking for ways of working together would be a good idea too! How about working with owners in 'similar' businesses to cooperate on staff training? I'm sure you can see reasons to justify joining forces in training staff in areas of common interest. It may be a bit of a challenge to get past the normal competitive urges. Leadership is about leverage not competition!

Good luck in your leadership, coaching and training efforts – your success depends on the decisions and actions you make in this regard. I hope this has been a helpful guide to making that success happen!

If I can be of assistance to you or you have some feedback or success stories to share, please email me personally at: bhooey@mcsnet.ca I'd be glad to hear from you, and to answer your questions where I can. Visit www.ideaman.net or www.BobHooey.training for more information.

Finding the TIME for training...

Continual training and professional development will allow your team the opportunity to realize their full potential. It pays off big dividends on better-equipped, energized team players on the job. As a leader or coach this can be your biggest obstacle in dealing with the 21st century challenges.

With increased demands on a smaller workforce, finding time for your team to attend training can be a challenge for most organizations. Applying some creativity and flexibility to your training program will yield powerful results

Here are some ideas to reduce classroom time, without jeopardizing the process of quality training:

Schedule team members to attend training between 10AM and 3PM, instead of a full day. In this case, they can still attend to urgent business. This works best for on-site training or training held very close to your operation. If training is off site, it might be better to start earlier. Perhaps splitting into two teams and run two ½ day sessions on the same day.

Weekend seminars are increasing in their popularity. Remember, if you ask your team to sacrifice their private time, be sure to include some group outing or a banquet to show your appreciation. Trade-off time during the week would be nice too! Respect and reward them!

Suggest your team study up on the course material in advance so they can hit the seminar running. We often provide some advance materials to facilitate this process when we work with out clients. Leverage the learning curve and enhance the application immediately.

How about scheduling a "lunch and learn" or "breakfast briefing with Bob," or inviting in a local expert when your team needs information on a simple topic. Combine a 'breakfast briefing' for management or specific team members in addition to a half-day or full-day training event.

Call 1-888-848-8407 (Toll Free North America) to leverage your training dollars and explore how to have Bob 'Idea Man' Hooey as part of your training and leadership success team, or as your personal HRD director.

How to avoid training mistakes...

As a leader, owner, manager, or coach, you frequently make decisions to engage, initiate, or contract programs and policies that will either help or hinder your team in reaching their goals. You can avoid making training mistakes by thinking ahead about a few ideas, and side stepping some of these mistakes that have minimized returns on training dollars.

Unfortunately, training time, resources, and dollars may be ultimately 'wasted' when leaders make any of the following mistakes.

Failing to fully assess team needs.

Perhaps you are teaching your team skills they already have? Team members don't need training 'just for the sake of training.' I've heard managers say, "Even if they know this stuff – a refresher won't hurt them?" Assess first then work on progress! Make it a positive choice!

Sometimes that is true (I've been asked back to reinforce a program or to provide add-on or follow-up sessions) – but if not handled correctly, it can be counter productive or a de-motivating event.

Here's a suggestion

Before you launch any training program, conduct a needs assessment with your team. Work to establish a comprehensive list of current team members' skills. This way, you may discover what they already know, and what they need (and hopefully want) to learn. Then, as you provide training it will send a positive message that you value their contributions and are dedicated to helping them increase and hone their skills. Ideas At Work! can help you design this assessment, and provide coaching and training for your success!

Thinking (wishfully) that training sessions will eliminate conflict.

Often managers think that training, especially training that focuses on team or relationship building, will help eliminate conflict on the job. Some programs over emphasize 'teamwork' at the expense of team effectiveness. All team efforts need to be focused, task and relationship oriented. When sessions focus too much on relationship building vs. team effectiveness, they lose impact, and can often become counter productive.

Here's a suggestion

Work to ensure everyone on your team knows that 'constructive' conflict is an important part of the team process. Without some conflict and honest difference of opinion you get mediocrity. As someone once told me *"the opposite of conflict is apathy, not peace and harmony."*

The secret is in not taking conflict as a personal issue, or a negative result in the process. Creative conflict can be a valid part of a positive process in making sure your team makes the best choice and fully explores all the options and potential pitfalls.

Thinking of training as a program vs. an ongoing process.

One of the challenges in training is the expectation that a half-day, full day or even a few days of training can change years of bad habits.

Research shows that shorter sessions spread over a longer time result in better retention and long-range effectiveness. Short and often rather than a one time massive attack seems to work. Projects have a beginning and an end. Processes are continual in their cycles and their ongoing effectiveness. We've been working on changing what we do for our clients. We've added additional pre-work to our training and designing in strategically spaced follow up and reinforcement to anchor their lessons.

Here's a suggestion

For your training to be effective, insights and ideas gained must be quickly translated into action (Ideas At Work!) – actions that are reinforced by the leaders on your team. Real development is never completed, as is the true essence of education – we keep learning!

In our training sessions, I challenge my audience members to make a serious commitment to act on what they learn, and to schedule those actions.

I hope these suggestions will help as you search out the most effective training programs for your team. I'd be happy to share some other thoughts with you if you have any other questions or queries.

How about other ideas or past mistakes that can be shared as lessons learned? I'd also be open to learning from your experiences in training your team. Drop me a note at: bob@ideaman.net

Accountability - key to effective meetings and leadership

How often have you sat in meetings listening to excuse after excuse from people who didn't do what they said they'd do at the last meeting? Does it bug you too? It does me!

One of the items I use personally to counteract this frustration, is an action list which summarizes what was agreed to be done, by who, and by when. This list, if kept and circulated to all in attendance immediately following the meeting makes people more accountable for their actions and in-actions. Two things will happen: 1) they will start doing more; or 2) they will stop talking and over-committing. Either way you win! Consider this for your coaching team. This idea works for leadership accountability too!

Here is a sample format for your use:

Date	Description of Action Completed	By Whom	Due	
d-m-y	what	Bob	d-m-y	y/n
d-m-y	what2	Sally	d-m-y	y/n

This simple tool can be very effective, if used properly and 'publicly' displayed. Just as it being the cornerstone of success teams, group accountability can push us to 'actually' complete that to which we commit ourselves.

If the reason for the meeting is important and vital to the success, growth, or other purposes of your organization or group -- don't you think the follow through is just as important? Accountability is the foundation of good leadership!

This is even more important in volunteer groups, where people come together under a common banner with individual agendas. The challenge is to blend those agendas to the common good and, having done that, to follow through and actually accomplish what has been talked about or agreed upon.

Don't be afraid to hold people accountable and set a higher standard. They will respond and follow through, or they will leave you free to accomplish that which is important. Either way, you win!

Seven Laws of Leadership

Here is a quick synopsis of my opening keynote session for 600 plus mayors, reeves and rural councillors in Edmonton, Alberta following the 2001 Alberta provincial election. Drawing from these Seven Laws of Leadership, I had the privilege of being selected to be the opening keynote for their convention following Lt. Governor Lois Hole.

There are basic tenants or laws that apply to being an effective and inspirational leader. With so many 'anti-heroes', and a demonstrated lack of leadership in so many branches of our government, our schools, and even our churches – people are seeking real leaders. They seek real leaders who can walk their talk and inspire them to greatness in their own lives.

Example – people need to be able to depend on your leadership
Today more than ever, people are looking for leaders who will lead by solid example in their dealings with people, and their lifestyles. We've grown to 'not' depend on people, and this is where you can 'differentiate' yourself.

Communication – people need to know what you are saying
Today more than ever, people are looking for clarity and consistency in our written and oral communications. They are looking for honesty and openness in the dialogue they have with us as leaders.

Ability – you need to be capable of leading other people
Today more than ever, people are looking for more than a slick appearance. They want content and proven ability they can trust to get them through the increasing challenges of the 21st Century.

Motivation – you need to know why you want to be a leader
Today more than ever, people want to know why you are doing what you are doing, and so do you! A simple trust me won't cut it. You need to be very clear in why you are taking on the leadership role if you hope to be successful in fulfilling it.

Authority – people need to respond to your leadership
Today more than ever, people want to be able to see demonstrated commitment, power in your decisions, and authority in your actions. People will respond if you are decisive and give good clear directions. Authority is not about being a 'boss', but in acting for the best interest of all.

Strategy/Vision – you need to know where you are going

Today more than ever, people want to know you have a plan -- one that is well thought out, covering all the contingencies and challenges. They want to know the relevant details of that strategy before they agree to follow you. If you are unclear or confused, those you hope to lead will be, too. Confusion leads to contention and a lack of commitment and follow through.

Love/Compassion – you need to care for the people around you

Today more than ever, people want to know you truly care about them, their needs, their concerns, their fears, their dreams, and their well-being. Lip service will not cut it on the 21st Century leadership track. This is perhaps the most important law, in that it must be demonstrated in your actions, your choice of words, and your life when you think no one is looking. If they see dishonesty or a lack of compassion, you will not win their loyalty or respect.

Take a serious look at your leadership skills considering the above seven laws. Those you would hope to lead are – and they are judging your actions, attitudes, and your motivation. They will follow, but you must be a leader!

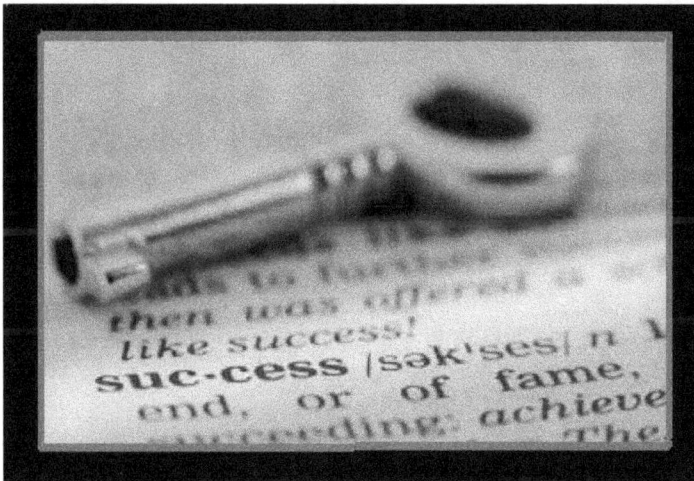

How do you measure up in relationship to these basic laws?

What do you have to change to become the leader you are needed to be, or have dreamed of being?

Bonus time: Write to me and share your insights after reading and applying these ideas. I'll send you a special article or two on leadership. Write me at: **bhooey@mcsnet.ca** and put "leadership article" in the subject line.

A Leader...

I went on a search to become a leader. I searched high and low. I spoke with authority. People listened. But alas, there was one who was wiser than I, and the crowd followed that individual.

I sought to inspire confidence, but the crowd responded, "Why should we trust you?" I postured, and I assumed the look of leadership with a countenance that flowed with confidence and pride. But many passed me by and never noticed my air of elegance.

I ran ahead of the others, pointed the way to new heights. I often demonstrated that I knew the route to greatness. And then I looked back, and I was alone. "What shall I do?" I queried. "I've tried hard and used all that I know." And I sat down and pondered long.

And then I listened to the voices around me. And I heard what the group was trying to accomplish. I rolled up my sleeves and joined in the work.

As we worked, I asked, "Are we all together in what we want to do and how to get the job done?"

I found myself encouraging the fainthearted. I sought the ideas of those too shy to speak out. I taught those who had little skill. I praised those who had worked hard. When our task was completed, one of the group turned to me and said, "This would not have been done but for your leadership."

At first, I said, "I didn't lead, I just worked with the rest." And then I understood, leadership is not a goal. It's a way of reaching a goal.

I lead best, when I help others to go where we've decided to go. **I lead best, when I help others to use themselves creatively.** *I lead best, when I forget about myself as a leader and focus on my group...their needs and their goals.*

Anonymous

28

Thanks for reading 'The Courage to Lead!'

Each time I prepare to step on the stage; each time I sit down to write or in this case to re-write, I am challenged to deliver something that will be of use-it-now value to my audiences.

I ask myself, *"If I was reading this, what value would I be looking for?"* As well, *"Why is this relevant to me, today?"*

Thanks for investing in yourself and this leadership workbook. These two questions help to keep me focused and clear on my objectives. They help to remind me to dig into my experiences, stories, examples, and research to provide solid information that will be of benefit and help our readers, when they apply it, succeed. That can be an exciting challenge!

I trust we have done that for you in this updated primer to enhance your sales skills. **'The Courage to Lead!'** is my attempt to capture some of the lessons learned first-hand from observing and working along side some tremendously effective leaders and to share them with you. I'd love to hear from you and read your success stories. If you would be so kind, please drop me a quick email at: bob@ideaman.net

Bob 'Idea Man' Hooey. Certified Virtual Presenter
2011 Spirit of CAPS recipient
www.ideaman.net
www.HaveMouthWillTravel.com

Connect with me on:
Facebook: www.facebook.com/bob.hooey
LinkedIn: www.linkedin.com/in/canadianideamanbobhooey
YouTube: www.youtube.com/ideamanbob
Smashwords: www.smashwords.com/PROfile/view/Hooey
Follow me on Twitter: @IdeamanHooey
Snail mail: Box 10, Egremont, Alberta T0A0Z0

About the author

Bob 'Idea Man' Hooey is a charismatic, confident leader, corporate trainer, inspiring facilitator, Emcee, prolific author, and award-winning motivational keynote speaker on leadership, creativity, success, business innovation, and enhancing team performance.

Using personal stories drawn from rich experience, he challenges his audiences to engage his **Ideas At Work!** – To act on what they hear, with clear, innovative building-blocks and field-proven success techniques to increase their effectiveness.

Bob challenges them to hone specific 'success skills' critical to their personal and professional advancement. Bob outlines real-life, results-based, innovative ideas personally drawn from 29 plus years of rich leadership experience in retail, construction, small business, entrepreneurship, manufacturing, association, consulting, community service, and commercial management.

Bob's conversational, often humorous, professional, and sometimes-provocative style continues to inspire and challenge his audiences across North America. Bob's motivational, innovative, challenging, and practical Ideas At Work! have been successfully applied by thousands of leaders and professionals across the globe.

Bob is a frequent contributor to North American consumer, corporate, association, trade, and on-line publications on leadership, success, employee motivation and training; as well as creativity and innovative problem solving, priority and time management, and effective customer service. He is the inspirational author of 30 plus publications, including several best-selling, print, e-books, reader style e-pubs, and a Pocket Wisdom series.

Visit: www.SuccessPublications.ca for more information.
Retired, award winning kitchen designer, Bob Hooey, CKD-Emeritus was one of only 75 Canadian designers to earn this prestigious certification by the National Kitchen and Bath Association.

In December 2000, Bob was given a special CAPS National Presidential award "…for his energetic contribution to the advancement of CAPS and **his living example of the power of one**" in addition to being elected to the CAPS National Board. He has been recognized by the National Speakers Association and other professional groups for his leadership contributions.

Bob is a co-founder and a past President of the CAPS Vancouver & BC Chapter and served as 2012 President of the CAPS Edmonton Chapter.

He is a member of the NSA-Arizona Chapter and an active leader in the National Speakers Association, a charter member of the Canadian Association of Professional Speakers, as well as the Global Speakers Federation (GSF). He retired (December 2013) as a Trustee from the CAPS Foundation. He is currently the CAPS GSF Ambassador.

In 1998, Toastmasters International recognized Bob "…for his professionalism and outstanding achievements in public speaking". That August in Palm Desert, California Bob became the 48th speaker in the world to be awarded this prestigious professional level honor as an Accredited Speaker. He has been inducted into their Hall of Fame on numerous occasions for his leadership contributions.

Bob has been honoured by the United Nations Association of BC (1993) and received the CANADA 125 award (1992) for his ongoing leadership contributions to the community. In 1998, Bob joined 3 other men to sail a 65-foot gaff rigged schooner from Honolulu, Hawaii to Kobe, Japan, barely surviving a 'baby' typhoon en-route.

In November 2011 Bob was awarded the Spirit of CAPS at their annual convention, becoming the 11th speaker to earn this prestigious CAPS National award. Visit: www.ideaman.net/SoC.htm

Bob pictured above presenting at the AFCP conference in Paris, France

Copyright and license notes

The Courage to Lead! (4th edition)
Idea-rich team empowerment strategies

Bob 'Idea Man' Hooey, Accredited Speaker, 2011 Spirit of CAPS recipient. Prolific author of 30 plus business, leadership, and career success publications

Unattributed quotations are by Bob 'Idea Man' Hooey.

Photos of Bob: **Dov Friedman**, www.photographybyDov.com
Photos of Bob: **Frédéric Bélot,** www.fredericbelot.fr/fr
Editorial, layout and design: **Irene Gaudet**, Vitrak Creative Services *(a division of Creativity Corner Inc.),* www.vitrakcreative.com

ISBN: 9781998014170

Success Publications – a division of Creativity Corner Inc.
Box 10, Egremont, AB T0A 0Z0
www.successpublications.ca
Creative office: 1-780-736-0009

Thank you for respecting the hard work of this author.

Acknowledgements, credits, and disclaimers

תודה
Dankie Gracias
Спасибо Merci شكرا Takk
Köszönjük   Terima kasih
Grazie Dziękujemy   Děkojame
Ďakujeme Vielen Dank Paldies
Kiitos Täname teid 谢谢

Thank You Tak

感謝您 Obrigado Teşekkür Ederiz
Σας Ευχαριστούμ 감사합니다
Bedankt Děkujeme vám
ありがとうございます
Tack

As with each of my books, a very special dedication of this piece of myself, to the two people who meant the most to me, my folks **Ron and Marge Hooey**. Sadly, both my parents left this earthly realm in 1999. I still miss our time together and your encouragement and love. I was blessed with the two of you in my life.

To my inspiring wife and professional proof-reader and publications coach, **Irene Gaudet**, who loves, encourages, and supports me in my quest to continue sharing my **Ideas At Work!** across the world. Thank you seems so inadequate for your timely work in helping make my writing and my client service better! I love the time we spend together!

My thanks to the many people who have encouraged me in my growth as a leader, speaker, and engaging trainer in each area of expertise including 'Courage to Lead'.

To my colleagues and friends in the National Speakers Association (NSA), the Canadian Association of Professional Speakers (CAPS), and the Global Speakers Federation (GSF) who continually challenge me to strive for success and increased excellence.

To my great audiences, leaders, students, coaching clients, and readers across the globe who share their experiences and enjoyment of my work. Your positive and supportive feedback encourages me to keep working on additional programs and success publications like this updated version. My experience with you creates the foundation for additional real-life experiences I can take from the stage to the page, the classroom to the boardroom.

My thanks to a select few friends for your ongoing support and 'constructive' abuse. You know who you are. ☺

Disclaimer

We have not attempted to cite all the authorities and sources consulted in the preparation of this book. To do so would require much more space than is available. The list would include departments of various governments, libraries, industrial institutions, periodicals, and many individuals. Inspiration was drawn from many sources, including other books by the author; in this updated creation of 'The Courage to Lead!'

This electronic mini book is written and designed to provide information on more effective use of your time, as a life and leadership enhancement guide. It is sold with the 'explicit' understanding that the publisher and/or the author are not engaged in rendering legal, accounting, or other professional services. If legal or other expert assistance is required, the services of a competent professional in your geographic area should be sought.

It is not the purpose of this book to reprint all the information that is otherwise available. Its primary purpose is to complement, amplify, and supplement other books and reference materials already available. You are encouraged to search out and study all the available material, learn as much as possible, and tailor the information to your individual needs. This will help to enhance your success in being a more effective salesperson, leader or professional.

Every effort has been made to make this book as complete and as accurate as possible within the scope of its focus. However, there may be mistakes, both typographical and in content or attribution. Graphics are royalty free or under license. Care has been taken to trace ownership of copyright material contained in this volume. The publisher will gladly receive information that will allow him to rectify any reference or credit line in subsequent editions. This book should be used only as a general guide and not as the ultimate source of information. Furthermore, this book contains information that is current only up to the date of publication.

The purpose of 'The Courage to Lead!' is to educate and entertain; perhaps to inform and to inspire. It is certainly to challenge its readers to learn and apply its secrets and tips, to challenge them to enhance their skills and leverage their time to create more productive outcomes. The author and publisher shall have neither liability nor responsibility to any person or entity with respect to any loss or damage caused, or alleged to have been caused, directly or indirectly, by the information contained in this book.

Bob's Publications

Bob is a prolific author who has been capturing and sharing his wisdom and experience in printed and electronic forms for the past twenty plus years. In addition to the following publications he has written for consumer, corporate, professional associations, trade, and on-line publications.

He has also been engaged to write and assist on publications by other writers and companies.

Leadership, business, and career development series

Running TOO Fast (8th edition 2022)
Legacy of Leadership (6th edition 2023)
Make ME Feel Special! (6th edition 2022)
Why Didn't I 'THINK' of That? (5th edition 2022)
Speaking for Success! (10th edition 2023)
THINK Beyond the First Sale (3rd edition 2022)
Prepare Yourself to Win! (3rd edition 2017)
The early years… 1998-2009 – A Tip of the Hat collection
The saga continues… 2010-2019 - A Tip of the Hat collection (2023)

Bob's Mini-book success series

The Courage to Lead! (4th edition 2023)
Creative Conflict (3rd edition 2017)
THINK Before You Ink! (3rd edition 2017)
Running to Win! (2nd edition 2017)
Generate More Sales (5thh edition 2023)
Unleash your Business Potential (3rd edition 2017)
Maximize Meetings (2019)
Learn to Listen (2nd edition 2020)
Creativity Counts! (2nd edition 2016)
Create Your Future! (3rd edition 2017)

Bob's Pocket Wisdom series
Pocket Wisdom for Speakers (updated 2023)

Pocket Wisdom for Leaders – Power of One! (2022)
Pocket Wisdom for Innovators – (2022)
More to be updated in 2024

Quick reads (2017-2023) - more to come

LEAD! *Idea-rich leadership success strategies*
CREATE! *Idea-rich strategies for enhanced innovation*
TIME! *Idea-rich tips for enhanced performance and productivity*
SERVE! *Idea-rich strategies for enhanced customer service*
SPEAK! *Idea-rich tips and techniques for great presentations*
CREATIVE CONFLICT *Idea-rich leadership for team success*
SUCCEED! *Idea-rich strategies to succeed in business, despite global disruptions* (2020)
WRITE ON! *Idea-rich tips and techniques to bring your book into pixels or print* (2020)
Get to Yes! *Idea-rich introductions to subtle art of creative persuasion in sales and negotiation* (2020)

Co-authored books created by Bob

Quantum Success – 3 volume series (2006)
In the Company of Leaders (95th anniversary Edition 2019)
Foundational Success (2nd Edition 2013)
PIVOT To Present: *Idea-rich strategies to deliver your virtual message with impact* (2020)

Visit: www.SuccessPublications.ca for more information

PRO-tips: Leaders, Managers, Owners

We'd suggest this book might be a great reference and discussion guide for you and your team. Work through it and discuss where it is relevant in your specific client interaction and culture. Working to create a client centered culture will pay dividends for years to come. We have **'The Courage to Lead!'** available as a lower investment E-pub version. Why not get each team member their own copy of the E-pub version? If you'd like to make a bulk order, please contact me and we'll work something out, just for you.

Email: bob@ideaman.net www.SuccessPublications.ca

What they say about Bob 'Idea Man' Hooey

As I travel across North America, and more recently around the globe, sharing my **Ideas At Work!,** I am fortunate to get feedback and comments from my audiences and colleagues. These comments come from people who have been touched, challenged, or simply enjoyed themselves in one of my sessions.

I'd love to come and share some ideas with your organization and teams.

"I've known Bob for several years and follow his activities in business with interest. I originally met Bob when he spoke for a Rotary Leadership Institute and got to know him better when he came to Vladivostok, Russia to speak to our leadership. When you spoke I thought you were one of us because you talked about our challenges just like yours. You could understand the others, which makes you a great speaker!" **Andrey Konyushok**, Rotary International District 2225 Governor 2012-2013, far eastern Russia

"I still get comments from people about your presentation. Only a few speakers have left an impression that lasts that long. You hit a spot with the tourism people." **Janet Bell**, Yukon Economic Forums

"We greatly appreciate the energy and effort you put into researching and adapting your keynote to make it more meaningful to our member councils. Early feedback from our delegates indicates that this year's convention was one of our most successful events yet, and we thank you for your contribution to this success." **Larry Goodhope**, Executive Director Alberta Association of Municipal Districts and Counties

"Thank you, Bob, it is always a pleasure to see a true professional at work. You have made the name 'Speaker' stand out as a truism - someone who encourages people to examine their lives and make adjustments. The personal stories you shared with your audience made such a great impression on everyone. The comments indicated you hit people right where it is important - in their hearts. Each of those in your audience took away a new feeling of personal success and encouragement." **Sherry Knight**, Dimension Eleven Human Resources and Communications

"Bob is one of those rare individuals who knows how to tackle obstacles in life to reach his dreams. He takes each as a learning experience and stretches for more. His compassion and genuine interest in others make him an exceptional coach."
Cindy Kindret, Training Manager, Silk FM Radio

"Without doubt, I have gained immeasurable self-assurance. Bob, your patience and your encouragement has been much appreciated. I strongly recommend your course to anyone looking for self-improvement and professional development." **Jeannie Mura**, Human Resources Chevron Canada

"I am pleased to recommend Bob 'Idea Man' Hooey to any organization looking for a charismatic, confident speaker and seminar leader. I have seen Bob in action on several occasions, and he is ALWAYS on! Bob has the ability to grab his audience's attention and keep it. Quite simply, if Bob is involved - your program or seminar is guaranteed to succeed." **Maurice Laving**, Coordinator Training and Development, London Drugs

"I have found Bob's attention to detail and his ability to fine tune his seminars to match the time frame and needs of the audience to be a valuable asset to our educational Program." **Patsy Schell**, Executive Director Surrey Chamber of Commerce

"Great seeing you in Cancun and congratulations on a job well done. The seminar was a great success! Your humorous and conversational style was a tremendous asset. It is my sincere hope that we can be associated again at future seminars." **Donald MacPherson**, Attorney At Law, Phoenix, Arizona

"What a great conference. It was a great pleasure meeting with you at the Ritz Carlton, Cancun and I shall look forward to hopefully welcoming you and your family in Dublin, Ireland someday." **A. Paul Ryan**, Petronva Corporation, Dublin, Ireland

"Congratulations on the Spirit of CAPS Award. You have worked long and hard on behalf of CAPS …helped many speakers including me and richly deserve this award. Well done my friend." **Peter Legge**, CSP, Hof, CPAE

"I had the pleasure of hearing and watching Bob Hooey deliver a keynote speech several years ago when he gave a presentation at a Toastmasters International Convention. Bob impressed me greatly with his professionalism, energy, and ability to connect with his audience while giving them value. Dr. **Dilip Abayasekara**, DTM, Accredited Speaker, Past Toastmasters International President

www.ingramcontent.com/pod-product-compliance
Lightning Source LLC
Chambersburg PA
CBHW071532210326
41597CB00018B/2973